SONNETS AND LYRICS

SONNETS AND LYRICS

BY

HELEN JACKSON (H. H.)

AUTHOR OF

"VERSES," "RAMONA," "BITS OF TRAVEL," ETC., ETC.

BOSTON
ROBERTS BROTHERS
1888

University Press:
JOHN WILSON AND SON, CAMBRIDGE.

UNTO one who lies at rest
'Neath the sunset, in the West,
Clover-blossoms on her breast.

Lover of each gracious thing
Which makes glad the summer-tide,
From the daisies clustering
And the violets purple-eyed,
To those shy and hidden blooms
Which in forest coverts stay,
Sending wandering perfumes
Out as guides to show the way,
All she knew, to all was kind;
None so humble or so small
That she did not seek and find
Silent friendship from them all.
Moss-cups, tiarella leaves,
Dappled like the adder's skin,
Fungus huts with ivory eaves
Which the fairies harbor in,
Regiments of fronded ferns,
Golden-rod and asters frail,
Every flaming leaf that burns
Red against the autumn pale,
Every pink-cupped wayside rose,—
All to her were dear and known;
But above them all she chose
Clover-blossoms for her own.

So they laid her to her rest
In the sun-warmed, bounteous West,
Clover-blossoms on her breast.

CONTENTS.

PAGE

A Dream 7

Danger 9

Freedom 10

The Gods said Love is Blind 11

The Fir-Tree and the Brook 12

A Rose-Leaf 14

A Woman's Battle 15

Esther 16

Vashti 17

Burnt Offering 18

Bon Voyage 20

New Year's Morning 21

January 23

February 24

March 25

April 26

May 27

PAGE

June 28
July 29
August 30
September 31
October 32
November 33
December 34
Refrain 35
To an Absent Lover 38
Crossed Threads 39
Outward Bound 40
Sealed Orders 41
Two 42
The Gift of Grapes 44
Avalanches 51
A Woman's Death-Wound 52
Chance 53
September 54
Appeal 56
Wreck 57
The Heart of a Rose 58
Acquainted with Grief 59
Fealty 61
Vision 62
The Poet's Forge 63
Vanity of Vanities 65

PAGE
Morn 67
Quatrains 68
Release 70
Where? 71
Emigravit 72
My Tenants 73
The Story of Boon 75
The Victory of Patience 94
God's Light-Houses 95
Songs of Battle 97
No Man's Land 98
Just out of Sight 100
September Woods 102
To-day 105
Opportunity 106
Flowers on a Grave 107
A Measure of Hours 109
Charlotte Cushman 112
Dedication 114
Dawn 115
Eve 115
Dreams 116
The Day-Star in the East 117
October's bright blue Weather 119
The Riviera 121
Semitones 122

PAGE
IN THE DARK 123
MORDECAI 124
IN APRIL 125
TWO HARVESTS 127
HABEAS CORPUS 129
A LAST PRAYER 132
THE SONG HE NEVER WROTE 133

A DREAM.

DREAMED that I was dead and crossed
the heavens, —
Heavens after heavens with burning feet
and swift, —
And cried: "O God, where art Thou? I left one
On earth, whose burden I would pray Thee lift."

I was so dead I wondered at no thing, —
Not even that the angels slowly turned
Their faces, speechless, as I hurried by
(Beneath my feet the golden pavements burned);

Nor, at the first, that I could not find God,
Because the heavens stretched endlessly like
space.
At last a terror seized my very soul;
I seemed alone in all the crowded place.

Then, sudden, one compassionate cried out,
  Though like the rest his face from me he turned,
As I were one no angel might regard
  (Beneath my feet the golden pavements burned):

"No more in heaven than earth will he find God
  Who does not know his loving mercy swift
But waits the moment consummate and ripe,
  Each burden from each human soul to lift."

Though I was dead, I died again for shame;
  Lonely, to flee from heaven again I turned;
The ranks of angels looked away from me
  (Beneath my feet the golden pavements burned).

DANGER.

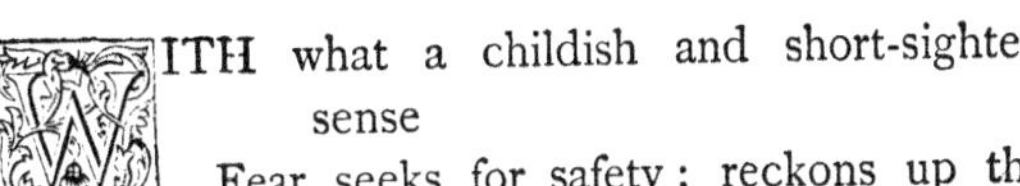

WITH what a childish and short-sighted sense
Fear seeks for safety; reckons up the days
Of danger and escape, the hours and ways
Of death; it breathless flies the pestilence;
It walls itself in towers of defence;
By land, by sea, against the storm it lays
Down barriers; then, comforted, it says:
"This spot, this hour is safe." Oh, vain pretence!
Man born of man knows nothing when he goes;
The winds blow where they list, and will disclose
To no man which brings safety, which brings risk.
The mighty are brought low by many a thing
Too small to name. Beneath the daisy's disk
Lies hid the pebble for the fatal sling.

FREEDOM.

HAT freeman knoweth freedom? Never he
Whose father's fathers through long lives have reigned
O'er kingdoms which mere heritage attained.
Though from his youth to age he roam as free
As winds, he dreams not freedom's ecstasy.
But he whose birth was in a nation chained
For centuries; where every breath was drained
From breasts of slaves which knew not there could be
Such thing as freedom, — he beholds the light
Burst, dazzling; though the glory blind his sight
He knows the joy. Fools laugh because he reels
And wields confusedly his infant will;
The wise man watching with a heart that feels
Says: "Cure for freedom's harms is freedom still."

THE GODS SAID LOVE IS BLIND.

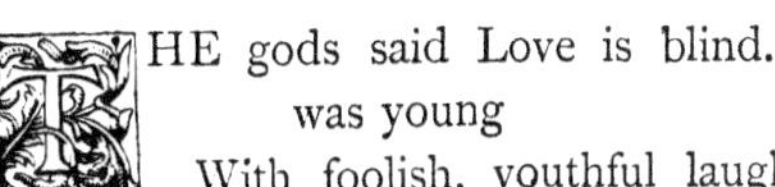

HE gods said Love is blind. The earth
was young
With foolish, youthful laughter when it
heard;
It caught and spoke the letter of the words,
And from that time till now hath said and sung,
"Oh, Love is blind! The falsest face and tongue
Can cheat him, once his passion's thrill is stirred:
He is so blind, poor Love!"
Strange none demurred
At this, nor saw how hollow false it rang,
When all men know that sightless men can tell
Unnumbered things which vision cannot find.
Powers of the air are leagued to guide them well;
And things invisible weave clew and spell
By which all labyrinths they safely wind.
Ah, we were lost, if Love had not been blind!

THE FIR-TREE AND THE BROOK.

THE Fir-Tree looked on stars, but loved the Brook!
"O silver-voiced! if thou wouldst wait,
My love can bravely woo." All smiles forsook
The Brook's white face. "Too late!
Too late! I go to wed the sea.
I know not if my love would curse or bless thee.
I may not, dare not, tarry to caress thee,
Oh, do not follow me!"

The Fir-Tree moaned and moaned till spring;
Then laughed in maniac joy to feel
Early one day, the woodmen of the King
Sign him with sign of burning steel,
The first to fall. "Now flee
Thy swiftest, Brook! Thy love may curse or bless me,
I care not, if but once thou dost caress me,
O Brook, I follow thee!"

All torn and bruised with mark of axe and chain,
Hurled down the dizzy slide of sand,

Tossed by great waves in ecstasy of pain,
And rudely thrown at last to land,
The Fir-Tree heard: "Oh, see
With what fierce love it is I must caress thee!
I warned thee I might curse, and never bless thee,
Why did'st thou follow me?"

All stately set with spar and brace and rope,
The Fir-Tree stood and sailed, and sailed.
In wildest storm when all the ship lost hope,
The Fir-Tree never shook nor quailed,
Nor ceased from saying, "Free
Art thou, O Brook! But once thou hast caressed me;
For life, for death, thy love has cursed or blessed me;
Behold, I follow thee!"

Lost in a night, and no man left to tell,
Crushed in the giant icebergs' play,
The ship went down without a song, a knell.
Still drifts the Fir-Tree night and day;
Still moans along the sea
A voice: "O Fir-Tree! thus must I possess thee;
Eternally, brave love, will I caress thee,
Dead for the love of me!"

A ROSE-LEAF.

ROSE-LEAF on the snowy deck,
  The high wind whirling it astern;
Nothing the wind could know or reck;
  Why did the King's eye thither turn?

"The Queen has walked here!" hoarse he cried.
  The courtiers, stunned, turned red, turned white;
No use if they had stammered, lied;
  Aghast they fled his angry sight.

Kings' wives die quick, when kings go mad;
  To death how fair and grave she goes!
What if the king knew now, she had
  Shut in her hand a little rose?

And men die quick when kings have said;
  Bleeding, dishonored, flung apart
In outcast field a man lies dead
  With rose-leaves warm upon his heart.

A WOMAN'S BATTLE.

DEAR foe, I know thou 'lt win the fight.
I know thou hast the stronger bark,
And thou art sailing in the light,
While I am creeping in the dark.
Thou dost not dream that I am crying,
As I come up with colors flying.

I clear away my wounded, slain,
With strength like frenzy, strong and swift;
I do not feel the tug and strain,
Though dead are heavy, hard to lift.
If I looked in their faces dying,
I could not keep my colors flying.

Dear foe, it will be short, — our fight, —
Though lazily thou train'st thy guns;
Fate steers us, — me to deeper night,
And thee to brighter seas and suns;
But thou 'lt not dream that I am dying,
As I sail by with colors flying!

ESTHER.

A FACE more vivid than he dreamed who
drew
Thy portrait in that thrilling tale of old!
Dead queen, we see thee still, thy beauty cold
As beautiful; thy dauntless heart which knew
No fear, — not even of a king who slew
At pleasure; maiden heart which was not sold,
Though all the maiden flesh the king's red gold
Did buy! The loyal daughter of the Jew,
No hour saw thee forget his misery;
Thou wert not queen until thy race went free;
Yet thoughtful hearts, that ponder slow and deep,
Find doubtful reverence at last for thee;
Thou heldest thy race too dear, thyself too cheap;
Honor no second place for truth can keep.

VASHTI.

N all great Shushan's palaces was there
Not one, O Vashti, knowing thee so well,
Poor uncrowned queen, that he the world could tell
How thou wert pure and loyal-souled as fair?
How it was love which made thee bold to dare
Refuse the shame which madmen would compel?
Not one, who saw the bitter tears that fell
And heard thy cry heart-rending on the air:
"Ah me! My Lord could not this thing have meant!
He well might loathe me ever, if I go
Before these drunken princes as a show.
I am his queen: I come of king's descent.
I will not let him bring our crown so low;
He will but bless me when he doth repent!"

BURNT OFFERING.

THE fire leaped up, swift, hot, and red;
Swift, hot, and red, waiting a prey;
The woman came with swift, light tread,
And silently knelt down to lay
Armfuls of leaves upon the fire,
As men lay fagots on a pyre.

Armfuls of leaves which had been bright
Like painter's tints six months before,
All faded now, a ghastly sight,
Dusty and colorless, she bore,
And knelt and piled them on the fire,
As men lay fagots on the pyre.

Watching the crackle and the blaze,
Idly I smiled and idly said:
"Good-by, dead leaves, go dead leaves' ways.
Next year there will be more as red."
The woman turned, and from the fire
Looked up as from a funeral-pyre.

I saw my idle words had been
Far crueler than I could know,
And made an old wound bleed again.
"These are not leaves," she whispered low,
"That I am burning in the fire,
But days, — it is a funeral pyre."

BON VOYAGE.

THERE 'S not an hour but from some sparkling beach
Go joyful men, in fragile ships to sail,
By unknown seas to unknown lands. They hail
The freshening winds with eager hope, and speech
Of wondrous countries which they soon will reach.
Left on the shore, we wave our hands, with pale,
Wet cheeks, but hearts that are ashamed to quail,
Or own the grief which selfishness would teach.
O Death, the fairest lands beyond thy sea
Lie waiting, and thy barks are swift and stanch
And ready. Why do we reluctant launch?
And when our friends their heritage have claimed
Of thee, and entered on it, rich and free,
Oh, why are we of sorrow not ashamed?

NEW YEAR'S MORNING.

NLY a night from old to new!
Only a night, and so much wrought!
The Old Year's heart all weary grew,
But said: "The New Year rest has brought."
The Old Year's heart its hopes laid down,
As in a grave; but, trusting, said:
"The blossoms of the New Year's crown
Bloom from the ashes of the dead."
The Old Year's heart was full of greed;
With selfishness it longed and ached,
And cried: "I have not half I need.
My thirst is bitter and unslaked.
But to the New Year's generous hand
All gifts in plenty shall return;
True loving it shall understand;
By all my failures it shall learn.
I have been reckless; it shall be
Quiet and calm and pure of life.
I was a slave; it shall go free,
And find sweet peace where I leave strife."

Only a night from old to new!
Never a night such changes brought.
The Old Year had its work to do;
No New Year miracles are wrought.

Always a night from old to new!
Night and the healing balm of sleep!
Each morn is New Year's morn come true,
Morn of a festival to keep.
All nights are sacred nights to make
Confession and resolve and prayer;
All days are sacred days to wake
New gladness in the sunny air.
Only a night from old to new;
Only a sleep from night to morn.
The new is but the old come true;
Each sunrise sees a new year born.

JANUARY.

WINTER! frozen pulse and heart of fire,
What loss is theirs who from thy kingdom turn
Dismayed, and think thy snow a sculptured urn
Of death! Far sooner in midsummer tire
The streams than under ice. June could not hire
Her roses to forego the strength they learn
In sleeping on thy breast. No fires can burn
The bridges thou dost lay where men desire
In vain to build.
O Heart, when Love's sun goes
To northward, and the sounds of singing cease,
Keep warm by inner fires, and rest in peace.
Sleep on content, as sleeps the patient rose.
Walk boldly on the white untrodden snows,
The winter is the winter's own release.

FEBRUARY.

TILL lie the sheltering snows, undimmed and white ;
And reigns the winter's pregnant silence still ;
No sign of spring, save that the catkins fill,
And willow stems grow daily red and bright.
These are the days when ancients held a rite
Of expiation for the old year's ill,
And prayer to purify the new year's will :
Fit days, ere yet the spring rains blur the sight,
Ere yet the bounding blood grows hot with haste,
And dreaming thoughts grow heavy with a greed
The ardent summer's joy to have and taste ;
Fit days, to give to last year's losses heed,
To reckon clear the new life's sterner need ;
Fit days, for Feast of Expiation placed !

MARCH.

MONTH which the warring ancients strangely styled
The month of war, — as if in their fierce ways
Were any month of peace! — in thy rough days
I find no war in Nature, though the wild
Winds clash and clang, and broken boughs are piled
At feet of writhing trees. The violets raise
Their heads without affright, without amaze,
And sleep through all the din, as sleeps a child.
And he who watches well may well discern
Sweet expectation in each living thing.
Like pregnant mother the sweet earth doth yearn;
In secret joy makes ready for the spring;
And hidden, sacred, in her breast doth bear
Annunciation lilies for the year.

APRIL.

NO days such honored days as these! While yet
Fair Aphrodite reigned, men seeking wide
For some fair thing which should forever bide
On earth, her beauteous memory to set
In fitting frame that no age could forget,
Her name in lovely April's name did hide,
And leave it there, eternally allied
To all the fairest flowers Spring did beget.
And when fair Aphrodite passed from earth,
Her shrines forgotten and her feasts of mirth,
A holier symbol still in seal and sign,
Sweet April took, of kingdom most divine,
When Christ ascended, in the time of birth
Of spring anemones, in Palestine.

MAY.

MONTH when they who love must love
and wed!
Were one to go to worlds where May is
naught,
And seek to tell the memories he had brought
From earth of thee, what were most fitly said?
I know not if the rosy showers shed
From apple-boughs, or if the soft green wrought
In fields, or if the robin's call be fraught
The most with thy delight. Perhaps they read
Thee best who in the ancient time did say
Thou wert the sacred month unto the old:
No blossom blooms upon thy brightest day
So subtly sweet as memories which unfold
In aged hearts which in thy sunshine lie,
To sun themselves once more before they die.

JUNE.

MONTH whose promise and fulfilment blend,
And burst in one! it seems the earth can store
In all her roomy house no treasure more;
Of all her wealth no farthing have to spend
On fruit, when once this stintless flowering end.
And yet no tiniest flower shall fall before
It hath made ready at its hidden core
Its tithe of seed, which we may count and tend
Till harvest. Joy of blossomed love, for thee
Seems it no fairer thing can yet have birth?
No room is left for deeper ecstasy?
Watch well if seeds grow strong, to scatter free
Germs for thy future summers on the earth.
A joy which is but joy soon comes to dearth.

JULY.

SOME flowers are withered and some joys
have died;
The garden reeks with an East Indian
scent
From beds where gillyflowers stand weak and spent;
The white heat pales the skies from side to side;
But in still lakes and rivers, cool, content,
Like starry blooms on a new firmament,
White lilies float and regally abide.
In vain the cruel skies their hot rays shed;
The lily does not feel their brazen glare.
In vain the pallid clouds refuse to share
Their dews; the lily feels no thirst, no dread.
Unharmed she lifts her queenly face and head;
She drinks of living waters and keeps fair.

AUGUST.

ILENCE again. The glorious symphony
Hath need of pause and interval of peace.
Some subtle signal bids all sweet sounds cease,
Save hum of insects' aimless industry.
Pathetic summer seeks by blazonry
Of color to conceal her swift decrease.
Weak subterfuge! Each mocking day doth fleece
A blossom, and lay bare her poverty.
Poor middle-agèd summer! Vain this show!
Whole fields of golden-rod cannot offset
One meadow with a single violet;
And well the singing thrush and lily know,
Spite of all artifice which her regret
Can deck in splendid guise, their time to go!

SEPTEMBER.

GOLDEN month! How high thy gold
is heaped!
The yellow birch-leaves shine like bright
coins strung
On wands; the chestnut's yellow pennons tongue
To every wind its harvest challenge. Steeped
In yellow, still lie fields where wheat was reaped;
And yellow still the corn sheaves, stacked among
The yellow gourds, which from the earth have wrung
Her utmost gold. To highest boughs have leaped
The purple grape, — last thing to ripen, late
By very reason of its precious cost.
O Heart, remember, vintages are lost
If grapes do not for freezing night-dews wait.
Think, while thou sunnest thyself in Joy's estate,
Mayhap thou canst not ripen without frost!

OCTOBER.

THE month of carnival of all the year,
When Nature lets the wild earth go its way,
And spend whole seasons on a single day.
The spring-time holds her white and purple dear;
October, lavish, flaunts them far and near;
The summer charily her reds doth lay
Like jewels on her costliest array;
October, scornful, burns them on a bier.
The winter hoards his pearls of frost in sign
Of kingdom: whiter pearls than winter knew,
Or Empress wore, in Egypt's ancient line,
October, feasting 'neath her dome of blue,
Drinks at a single draught, slow filtered through
Sunshiny air, as in a tingling wine!

NOVEMBER.

THIS is the treacherous month when autumn days
With summer's voice come bearing summer's gifts.
Beguiled, the pale down-trodden aster lifts
Her head and blooms again. The soft, warm haze
Makes moist once more the sere and dusty ways,
And, creeping through where dead leaves lie in drifts,
The violet returns. Snow noiseless sifts
Ere night, an icy shroud, which morning's rays
Will idly shine upon and slowly melt,
Too late to bid the violet live again.
The treachery, at last, too late, is plain;
Bare are the places where the sweet flowers dwelt.
What joy sufficient hath November felt?
What profit from the violet's day of pain?

DECEMBER.

HE lakes of ice gleam bluer than the lakes
Of water 'neath the summer sunshine gleamed:
Far fairer than when placidly it streamed,
The brook its frozen architecture makes,
And under bridges white its swift way takes.
Snow comes and goes as messenger who dreamed
Might linger on the road; or one who deemed
His message hostile gently for their sakes
Who listened might reveal it by degrees.
We gird against the cold of winter wind
Our loins now with mighty bands of sleep,
In longest, darkest nights take rest and ease,
And every shortening day, as shadows creep
O'er the brief noontide, fresh surprises find.

REFRAIN.

OF all the songs which poets sing,
The ones which are most sweet,
Are those which at close intervals
A low refrain repeat;
Some tender word, some syllable,
Over and over, ever and ever,
While the song lasts,
Altering never,
Music if sung, music if said,
Subtle like some fine golden thread
A shuttle casts,
In and out on a fabric red,
Till it glows all through
With the golden hue.
Oh! of all the songs sung,
No songs are so sweet
As the songs with refrains,
Which repeat and repeat.

Of all the lives lived,
No life is so sweet,

As the life where one thought,
In refrain doth repeat,
Over and over, ever and ever,
Till the life ends,
Altering never,
Joy which is felt, but is not said,
Subtler than any golden thread
Which the shuttle sends
In and out in a fabric red,
Till it glows all through
With a golden hue.
Oh! of all the lives lived,
Can be no life so sweet
As the life where one thought
In refrain doth repeat.

"Now name me a thought
To make life so sweet,
A thought of such joy
Its refrain to repeat."
Oh! foolish to ask me. Ever, ever
Who loveth believes,
But telleth never.
It might be a name, just a name not said,
But in every thought; like a golden thread
Which the shuttle weaves
In and out on a fabric red,

Till it glows all through
With a golden hue.
Oh! of all sweet lives,
Who can tell how sweet
Is the life which one name
In refrain doth repeat?

TO AN ABSENT LOVER.

THAT so much change should come when thou dost go,
Is mystery that I cannot ravel quite.
The very house seems dark as when the light
Of lamps goes out. Each wonted thing doth grow
So altered, that I wander to and fro
Bewildered by the most familiar sight,
And feel like one who rouses in the night
From dream of ecstasy, and cannot know
At first if he be sleeping or awake.
My foolish heart so foolish for thy sake
Hath grown, dear one!
Teach me to be more wise.
I blush for all my foolishness doth lack;
I fear to seem a coward in thine eyes.
Teach me, dear one, — but first thou must come back!

CROSSED THREADS.

THE silken threads by viewless spinners
spun,
Which float so idly on the summer air,
And help to make each summer morning fair,
Shining like silver in the summer sun,
Are caught by wayward breezes, one by one,
And blown to east and west and fastened there,
Weaving on all the roads their sudden snare.
No sign which road doth safest, freest run,
The wingèd insects know, that soar so gay
To meet their death upon each summer day.
How dare we any human deed arraign ;
Attempt to reckon any moment's cost ;
Or any pathway trust as safe and plain
Because we see not where the threads have crossed?

OUTWARD BOUND.

HE hour has come. Strong hands the anchor raise;
Friends stand and weep along the fading shore,
In sudden fear lest we return no more,
In sudden fancy that he safer stays
Who stays behind; that some new danger lays
New snare in each fresh path untrod before.
Ah, foolish hearts! in fate's mysterious lore
Is written no such choice of plan and days:
Each hour has its own peril and escape;
In most familiar things' familiar shape
New danger comes without or sight or sound;
No sea more foreign rolls than breaks each morn
Across our thresholds when the day is born:
We sail, at sunrise, daily, "outward bound."

SEALED ORDERS.

WHEN ship with "orders sealed" sails out
to sea,
Men eager crowd the wharves, and rev-
erent gaze
Upon their faces whose brave spirits raise
No question if the unknown voyage be
Of deadly peril. Benedictions free
And prayers and tears are given, and the days
Counted till other ships, on homeward ways,
May bring back message of her destiny.
Yet, all the time, Life's tossing sea is white
With scudding sails which no man reefs or stays
By his own will, for roughest day or night:
Brave, helpless crews, with captain out of sight,
Harbor unknown, voyage of long delays,
They meet no other ships on homeward ways.

TWO.

I.

APART.

ONE place — one roof — one name — their
daily bread
In daily sacrament they break
Together, and together take
Perpetual counsel, such as use has fed
The habit of, in words which make
No lie. For courtesy's sweet sake
And pity's, one brave heart whose joy is dead,
Smiles ever, answering words which wake
But weariness; hides all its ache, —
Its hopeless ache, its longing and its dread;
Strong as a martyr at the stake
Renouncing self; striving to slake
The pangs of thirst on bitter hyssop red
With vinegar! O brave, strong heart!
God sets all days, all hours apart,
Joy cometh at his hour appointed.

II.

TOGETHER.

No touch — no sight — no sound — wide continents
And seas clasp hands to separate
Them from each other now. Too late!
Triumphant Love has leagued the elements
To do their will. Hath light a mate
For swiftness? Can it overweight
The air? Or doth the sun know accidents?
The light, the air, the sun, inviolate
For them, do constant keep and state
Message of their ineffable contents
And raptures, each in each. So great
Their bliss of loving, even fate
In parting them, hath found no instruments
Whose bitter pain insatiate
Doth kill it, or their faith abate
In presence of Love's hourly sacraments.

THE GIFT OF GRAPES.

A LEGEND OF THE FOURTH CENTURY.

HE desert sun was sinking red;
Hot as at noon the light was shed.

Bareheaded, on the scorching sands,
Macarius knelt with claspèd hands,

And prayed, as he had prayed for years,
With smitings and with bitter tears.

"Good hermit, here!" — a hand outstretched, —
It was as if an angel fetched

The purple clusters, dewy blue, —
"Good hermit, here! These grapes for you!"

Swift swept the rider by. The grapes
Lay at the hermit's feet. "Like shapes

"Of magic, sent to tempt my sense,"
Macarius thought. "Sathanas, hence!"

He cried. "I will not touch nor taste.
Yet, were it not wrong such fruit to waste?"

He paused. "I'll leave it at his door,
My neighbor, who with illness sore

"Is like to die. He may partake,
And sin not. Ay, for Jesus' sake,

"I will his dying lips beseech,
Command, as if I were his leech."

Thus speaking, trembling as he spoke,
Such parched desire within him woke,

To taste the grapes, he swiftly ran,
And, kneeling by the dying man,

Held up the clusters, crying, "See,
O brother! these were given me.

"I may not eat them; I am strong;
But thou — it were for thee no wrong.

"Thy fever they will cool, allay;
Thy failing strength revive and stay."

Reproachful turned the dying eyes,
The whispers came like dying sighs:

"Brother, thou mightst do better deed
Than tempt the dying in his need.

"Thy words are but the devil's mesh,
To snare at last my carnal flesh."

Silent, Macarius went his way.
Untouched the purple clusters lay

Beside the dying hermit's bed.
They found them there who found him dead, —

Two brother hermits who each morn,
Water and bread to him had borne.

"He drinks of living waters now,"
They pious said, and smoothed his brow,

And prayed, and laid him in the ground,
Envying the rest he had found.

The purple grapes still lying there,
Filled with sweet scent the desert air.

"Where could these luscious clusters grow?"
"He tasted not," they whispered low;

"But fairer fruit glads now his eyes:
He feasts to-day in paradise."

On each a longing silence fell.
" Brother, they tempt our souls to hell ! "

Cried one. The other : " Ay, how weak
Our flesh ! Strange that so long we seek

" In vain to dull its carnal sense.
Brother, we 'll bear these clusters hence.

" That aged hermit, in the cave,
Perchance these grapes his life might save.

" Thou knowest, but yesterday 't was said
He starves ; eats neither pulse nor bread."

Slow braiding baskets, in his door
The aged hermit sat, his store

Of rushes and his water-jar
In reach. He heard their steps afar,

And, as they nearer drew, up-raised
His well-nigh sightless eyes, and gazed

Bewilderedly. " Eat, father, eat ! "
The brothers cried, and at his feet,

Rev'rent, the purple clusters laid.
Trembling, but stern, the right hand made

Swift gesture of reproof. "Away!"
In feeble voice he cried, "and pray

"To be forgiven! Heinous sin
Is his who lets temptation in."

Meek-bowed, the brothers turned to go.
"Stay!" said the hermit, whispering low:

"Leave them not here to tempt my sight.
I may not eat. Some other night.

"As each man thinketh in his heart,
So must he reckon duty's part.

"Mayhap some brother, in sore strait,
Even this hour doth sit and wait,

"To whom God sends these clusters sweet
By your pure hands. Be true! Be fleet!"

From cave to cave, from cell to cell,
The brothers did their errand well.

In Nitria's desert, hermits then
By scores were dwelling, holy men,

Mistaken saints, who thought to save
Their souls, by making life a grave.

From cave to cave, from cell to cell,
The brothers did their errand well.

At every hermit's feet they laid
The tempting grapes, in vain, nor stayed

Till, at the desert's utmost bound,
Macarius's cell they joyful found, —

Macarius, oldest, holiest saint
Of all the desert. Weary, faint,

They knelt before him. " Father, see
These grapes ! they must be meant for thee !

" These many days we bear them now ;
And yet they do not withered grow.

" No brother will so much as taste.
'T was Isidore who bade us haste

" To find the man to whom God sent
The luscious gift. They must be meant

" For thee. Thou art the last." " Ay," said
The good Macarius, flushing red

With holy joy, — " Ay ; meant for me,
As token of the constancy

"Of all our brothers! Blessed day
Is this, my brothers! Go your way!

"Christ fill your souls with lasting peace!
The time is near of my release."

Then, kneeling on the scorching sands,
He stretched toward heaven his claspèd hands,

And prayed, as he had prayed for years,
With smitings and with bitter tears.

Untouched, the grapes lay glowing there,
Filling with scent the desert air.

AVALANCHES.

O HEART that on Love's sunny height doth
 dwell,
And joy unquestioning by day, by night,
Serene in trust because the skies are bright!
Listen to what all Alpine records tell
Of days on which the avalanches fell.
Not days of storm when men were pale with fright,
And watched the hills with anxious, straining sight,
And heard in every sound a note of knell;
But when in heavens still, and blue, and clear,
The sun rode high, — those were the hours to fear.
And so the monks of San Bernard to-day, —
May the Lord count their souls and hold them dear, —
When skies are cloudless, in their convent stay,
And for the souls of dead and dying pray.

A WOMAN'S DEATH-WOUND.

T left upon her tender flesh no trace.
The murderer is safe. As swift as light
The weapon fell, and, in the summer night,
Did scarce the silent, dewy air displace;
'T was but a word. A blow had been less base.
Like dumb beast branded by an iron white
With heat, she turned in blind and helpless flight,
But then remembered, and with piteous face
Came back.
Since then, the world has nothing missed
In her, in voice or smile. But she — each day
She counts until her dying be complete.
One moan she makes, and ever doth repeat:
" O lips that I have loved and kissed and kissed,
Did I deserve to die this bitterest way? "

CHANCE.

THESE things I wondering saw beneath the sun:
That never yet the race was to the swift,
The fight unto the mightiest to lift,
Nor favors unto men whose skill had done
Great works, nor riches ever unto one
Wise man of understanding. All is drift
Of time and chance, and none may stay or sift
Or know the end of that which is begun.
Who waits until the wind shall silent keep,
Will never find the ready hour to sow.
Who watcheth clouds will have no time to reap.
At daydawn plant thy seed, and be not slow
At night. God doth not slumber take nor sleep:
Which seed shall prosper thou canst never know.

SEPTEMBER.

HE golden-rod is yellow;
  The corn is turning brown;
The trees in apple orchards
  With fruit are bending down.

The gentian's bluest fringes
  Are curling in the sun;
In dusty pods the milkweed
  Its hidden silk has spun.

The sedges flaunt their harvest,
  In every meadow nook;
And asters by the brook-side
  Make asters in the brook.

From dewy lanes at morning
  The grapes' sweet odors rise;
At noon the roads all flutter
  With yellow butterflies.

By all these lovely tokens
  September days are here,
With summer's best of weather,
  And autumn's best of cheer.

But none of all this beauty
  Which floods the earth and air
Is unto me the secret
  Which makes September fair.

'T is a thing which I remember;
  To name it thrills me yet:
One day of one September
  I never can forget.

APPEAL.

"  LOVE, whom I so love, in this sore strait
Of thine, fail not! Below thy very feet
I kneel, so much I reverence thee, so sweet
It is to every pulse of mine to wait
Thy lightest pleasure, and to bind my fate
To thine by humblest service. Incomplete
All heaven, Love, if there thou dost not greet
Me, with perpetual need which I can sate,
I and no other! So I dare to pray
To thee this prayer. It is not wholly prayer.
The solemn worships of the ages lay
Even on God a solemn bond. I dare, —
Thy worshipper, thy lowly, loving mate, —
I dare to say, O Love, thou must be great!"

THE HEART OF A ROSE.

ROSE like a hollow cup with a brim, —
A brim as pink as the after-glow ;
Deep down in its heart gold stamens swim,
Tremble and swim in a sea of snow.
My Love set it safe in a crystal glass,
Gently as petals float down at noon.
Low, in a whisper, my Love's voice said :
"Look quick ! In an hour it will be dead.
I picked it because it will die so soon.
Now listen, dear Heart, as the seconds pass,
What the rose will say," my Love's voice said.

I look and I listen. The flushed pink brim
Is still as June's warmest after-glow ;
Silent as stars the gold stamens swim,
Tremble and swim in their sea of snow.
I dare not breathe on the crystal glass,
Lest one sweet petal should fall too soon.
False was the whisper my Love's voice said, —
If he had not picked it, it had been dead ;
But now it will live an eternal noon,
And I shall hear as the seconds pass
What the rose will say till I am dead.

ACQUAINTED WITH GRIEF.

DOST know Grief well? Hast known her
long?
So long, that not with gift or smile,
Or gliding footstep in the throng,
She can deceive thee by her guile?

So long, that with unflinching eyes
Thou smilest to thyself apart,
To watch each flimsy, fresh disguise
She plans to stab anew thy heart?

So long, thou barrest up no door
To stay the coming of her feet?
So long, thou answerest no more,
Lest in her ear thy cry be sweet?

Dost know the voice in which she says,
" No more henceforth our paths divide;
In loneliest nights, in crowded days,
I am forever by thy side"?

ACQUAINTED WITH GRIEF.

DOST know Grief well? Hast known her
long?
So long, that not with gift or smile,
Or gliding footstep in the throng,
She can deceive thee by her guile?

So long, that with unflinching eyes
Thou smilest to thyself apart,
To watch each flimsy, fresh disguise
She plans to stab anew thy heart?

So long, thou barrest up no door
To stay the coming of her feet?
So long, thou answerest no more,
Lest in her ear thy cry be sweet?

Dost know the voice in which she says,
"No more henceforth our paths divide;
In loneliest nights, in crowded days,
I am forever by thy side"?

Then dost thou know, perchance, the spell
The gods laid on her at her birth, —
The viewless gods who mingle well
Strange love and hate of us on earth.

Weapon and time, the hour, the place,
All these are hers to take, to choose,
To give us neither rest nor grace,
Not one heart-throb to miss or lose.

All these are hers; yet stands she, slave,
Helpless before our one behest:
The gods, that we be shamed not, gave,
And locked the secret in our breast.

She to the gazing world must bear
Our crowns of triumph, if we bid;
Loyal and mute, our colors wear,
Sign of her own forever hid.

Smile to our smile, song to our song,
With songs and smiles our roses fling,
Till men turn round in every throng,
To note such joyous pleasuring,

And ask, next morn, with eyes that lend
A fervor to the words they say,
"What is her name, that radiant friend
Who walked beside you yesterday?"

FEALTY.

HE thing I count and hold as fealty —
The only fealty to give or take —
Doth never reckoning keep, and coldly make
Bond to itself with this or that to be
Content as wage ; the wage unpaid, to free
Its hand from service, and its love forsake,
Its faith cast off, as one from dreams might wake
At morn, and smiling watch the vision flee.
Such fealty is treason in disguise.
Who trusts it, his death-warrant sealed doth bear.
Love looks at it with angry, wondering eyes ;
Love knows the face true fealty doth wear,
The pulse that beats unchanged by alien air,
Or hurts, or crimes, until the loved one dies.

VISION.

Y subtile secrets of discovered law
Men well have measured the horizon's round,
Kept record of the speed of light and sound,
Have close defined by reasoning without flaw
The utmost human vision ever saw
Unaided, and have arrant sought and found
Devices countless to extend its bound.
Bootless their secrets all! My eyes but stray
To eastward, and majestic, bright, arise
Peaks of a range which three days distant lies!
And of the faces, too, that light my day
Most clear, one is a continent away,
The other shines above the farthest skies!

THE POET'S FORGE.

HE lies on his back, the idling smith,
  A lazy, dreaming fellow is he;
The sky is blue, or the sky is gray,
He lies on his back the livelong day,
Not a tool in sight; say what they may,
  A curious sort of a smith is he.

The powers of the air are in league with him;
  The country around believes it well;
The wondering folk draw spying near;
Never sight nor sound do they see or hear;
No wonder they feel a little fear;
  When is it his work is done so well?

Never sight nor sound to see or hear;
  The powers of the air are in league with him;
High over his head his metals swing,
Fine gold and silver to shame the king;
We might distinguish their glittering,
  If once we could get in league with him.

High over his head his metals swing;
He hammers them idly year by year,
Hammers and chuckles a low refrain:
"A bench and book are a ball and chain,
The adze is better tool than the plane;
What 's the odds between now and next year?"

Hammers and chuckles his low refrain,
A lazy, dreaming fellow is he:
When sudden, some day, his bells peal out,
And men, at the sound, for gladness shout;
He laughs and asks what it 's all about;
Oh, a curious sort of smith is he!

VANITY OF VANITIES.

EE to the blossom, moth to the flame;
Each to his passion; what 's in a name?

Red clover 's sweetest, well the bee knows;
No bee can suck it; lonely it blows.

Deep lies its honey, out of reach, deep;
What use in honey hidden to keep?

Robbed in the autumn, starving for bread;
Who stops to pity a honey-bee dead?

Star-flames are brightest, blazing the skies;
Only a hand's-breadth the moth-wing flies.

Fooled with a candle, scorched with a breath;
Poor little miller, a tawdry death!

Life is a honey, life is a flame;
Each to his passion; what 's in a name?

Swinging and circling, face to the sun,
Brief little planet, how it doth run!

Bee-time and moth-time, add the amount;
White heat and honey, who keeps the count?

Gone some fine evening, a spark out-tost!
The world no darker for one star lost!

Bee to the blossom, moth to the flame;
Each to his passion; what 's in a name?

MORN.

N what a strange bewilderment do we
Awake each morn from out the brief night's sleep.
Our struggling consciousness doth grope and creep
Its slow way back, as if it could not free
Itself from bonds unseen. Then Memory,
Like sudden light, outflashes from its deep
The joy or grief which it had last to keep
For us; and by the joy or grief we see
The new day dawneth like the yesterday;
We are unchanged; our life the same we knew
Before. I wonder if this is the way
We wake from death's short sleep, to struggle through
A brief bewilderment, and in dismay
Behold our life unto our old life true.

QUATRAINS.

THE MONEY-SEEKER.

WHAT has he in this glorious world's domain?
Unreckoned loss which he counts up for gain,
Unreckoned shame, of which he feels no stain,
Unreckoned dead he does not know were slain.

What things does he take with him when he dies?
Nothing of all that he on earth did prize:
Unto his grovelling feet and sordid eyes
How difficult and empty seem the skies!

THE LOVER.

HE knows the utmost secret of the earth:
The golden sunrise's and sunset's worth;
The pregnancy of every blossom's birth;
The hidden name of every creature's mirth.

He knows all measures of the pulse's beat;
He knows all pathless paths of human feet;
He knows what angels know not of the sweet
Fulfilments when love's being is complete.

He knows all deadly soils where poisons bloom;
He knows the fated road where joy makes room
For nameless terrors and eternal gloom:
God help him in his sad omniscient doom!

RELEASE.

F one had watched a prisoner many a year,
Standing behind a barrèd window-pane,
Fettered with heavy handcuff and with chain,
And gazing on the blue sky, far and clear;
And suddenly some morning he should hear
The man had in the night contrived to gain
His freedom and was safe, would this bring pain?
Ah! would it not to dullest heart appear
Good tidings?
Yesterday I looked on one
Who lay as if asleep in perfect peace.
His long imprisonment for life was done.
Eternity's great freedom his release
Had brought. Yet they who loved him called him dead,
And wept, refusing to be comforted.

WHERE?

MY snowy eupatorium has dropped
Its silver threads of petals in the night;
No signal told its blossoming had stopped;
Its seed-films flutter silent, ghostly white:
No answer stirs the shining air,
As I ask, "Where?"

Beneath the glossy leaves of winter-green
Dead lily-bells lie low, and in their place
A rounded disk of pearly pink is seen,
Which tells not of the lily's fragrant grace:
No answer stirs the shining air,
As I ask, "Where?"

This morning's sunrise does not show to me
Seed-film or fruit of my sweet yesterday;
Like falling flowers, to realms I cannot see
Its moments floated silently away:
No answer stirs the shining air,
As I ask, "Where?"

EMIGRAVIT.

ITH sails full set, the ship her anchor weighs.
Strange names shine out beneath her figure head.
What glad farewells with eager eyes are said!
What cheer for him who goes, and him who stays!
Fair skies, rich lands, new homes, and untried days
Some go to seek; the rest but wait instead
Until the next stanch ship her flag doth raise.
Who knows what myriad colonies there are
Of fairest fields, and rich, undreamed-of gains
Thick planted in the distant shining plains
Which we call sky because they lie so far?
Oh, write of me, not "Died in bitter pains,"
But "Emigrated to another star!"

MY TENANTS.

NEVER had a title-deed
To my estate. But little heed
Eyes give to me, when I walk by
My fields, to see who occupy.
Some clumsy men who lease and hire
And cut my trees to feed their fire,
Own all the land that I possess,
And tax my tenants to distress.
And if I said I had been first,
And, reaping, left for them the worst,
That they were beggars at the hands
Of dwellers on my royal lands,
With idle laugh of passing scorn
As unto words of madness born,
They would reply.
I do not care;
They cannot crowd the charmèd air;
They cannot touch the bonds I hold
On all that they have bought and sold.
They can waylay my faithful bees,
Who, lulled to sleep, with fatal ease,

Are robbed. Is one day's honey sweet
Thus snatched? All summer round my feet
In golden drifts from plumy wings,
In shining drops on fragrant things,
Free gift, it came to me. My corn,
With burnished banners, morn by morn,
Comes out to meet and honor me;
The glittering ranks spread royally
Far as I walk. When hasty greed
Tramples it down for food and seed,
I, with a certain veiled delight,
Hear half the crop is lost by blight.
  Letter of law these may fulfil,
Plant where they like, slay what they will,
Count up their gains and make them great;
Nevertheless, the whole estate
Always belongs to me and mine.
We are the only royal line.
And though I have no title-deed
My tenants pay me loyal heed
When our sweet fields I wander by
To see what strangers occupy.

THE STORY OF BOON.[1]

IT haunts my thoughts morn, night, and
noon,
The story of the woman, Boon, —
Haunts me like restless ghost, until
I give myself to do its will;
Cries voiceless, yet as voices cry, —
"O singer, can this tale pass by
Untold by thee? Thy heart is wrung
In vain, if dies the song unsung."
I am unworthy: master hands
Should strike the chords, and fill the lands
From sea to sea with melody
All reverent, yet with harmony
Majestic, jubilant, to tell
How love must love, if love loves well;
How once incarnate love was found
On earth, dishonored, martyr-crowned,
Crowned by a heathen woman's name, —
O blessed Boon, of peerless fame!

1 This story of Boon is strictly true. It is told by Mrs. Leonowens, the English Governess at the Siamese court. She took it down from Choy's own lips.

In Siam's court the Buddhist King
Held festival. Fair girls to sing,
And dance, and play, were led between
Close ranks of Amazons in green
And gold. In chariot milk-white
Of ivory, and glittering bright
With flowers garlanded, rode Choy,
The young, the beautiful; with joy
And subtle pride no words could tell,
Her virgin bosom rose and fell.
No dream the Siam maiden knew
More high or blest than that which grew
In Choy's poor blinded heart, — to be
The favorite of the King, and see
The other wives beneath her feet.
From babyhood, that this was sweet
The child was taught. How should she know
They told her false, and worked her woe!

The song, the dance, the play, were done,
Choy's fatal triumph had been won.
The old king's bleared and lustful eyes
Had marked her for his next new prize.
Asking her name, as low she bowed
Before the throne, he called aloud, —
"Which of my nobles springs to lead
Her chariot ponies? Do I need
Speak farther?"
On the instant, two
Young nobles robed in white sprang through

The crowd, and kneeling as to queen,
With low-bent head and reverent mien,
They walked the chariot beside.
The bands burst forth in swelling tide
Of music, and the curtain fell.
One noble, smitten by the spell
Of Choy's great beauty, whispered, " God,
How beautiful thou art!"
"My Lord,
Have care," the scornful Choy exclaimed:
"'T were ill for thee, if thou wert blamed
By me."
The other noble silent gazed,
With eyes whose glance strange tumult raised
Within Choy's breast. He did not speak:
All spoken words had fallen weak,
After his look. Yet Choy's heart burned
To hear his voice. Sudden she turned,
And leaning forward said, " How now,
What seest thou in air that thou
Art dumb?"
With trembling lips he spoke, —
"O Lady, till thy sweet voice broke
Upon the air, I thought I saw
An angel; now, with no less awe,
But greater joy, I see thou art
A woman."
Ah, they know not heart

Of man or woman, who declare
That love needs time to love and dare.
His altars wait, — not day nor name,
Only the touch of sacred flame.

The song, the dance, the play were done.
Oh, fatal triumph Choy had won!
Oh, hateful life she thought was sweet!
She knelt before the old king's feet,
A slave, a toy, a purchased thing,
Which to his worn-out sense might bring
Pleasure again of touch, of sight.
Doting, he named her "Chorm," "Delight,"
Decked her with jewels, gave her power,
And day and night, and hour by hour,
With hideous caresses sought
Joy in the thing which he had bought.
And hour by hour, and night and day,
Wasted poor Choy's young life away.
One thrilling voice, one glowing face,
One thought of such a love's embrace,
Haunted her thoughts, and racked her breast,
Robbed her of peace, robbed her of rest,
Made of her life such living lie,
Such torture, she but prayed to die.

Months passed, and she knew not the name
Of him she loved. At last there came

The fated day. A woman slave,
New in the palace, quickly gave,
Answering Choy's artful questioning,
The noble's name.
"Ah, go and bring
Me news of him," said Choy. "He bore
Himself so loftily, I more
Recall him than all else that day.
Seek out minutely in what way
He lives; what may his harem hold.
He seemed to me so silent, cold,
No doubt some Houri keeps him chained,"
With scornful laugh, but poorly feigned,
Cried Choy.
At dusk of night returned
The slave, with wondrous tale, which burned
Itself on Choy's glad heart.
The Duke,
Phaya Phi Chitt his name, forsook
His harem on the day he led
The Favorite's chariot ponies. Dead
He seemed to all he once had loved:
No fear, no joy, his spirit moved.
His friends believed that he was mad,
Or else some mortal illness had.
A feverish joy filled all Choy's thought,
She knew by what this change was wrought.
Love's keenest pain, if shared like this,
No longer seemed a pain, but bliss.

Again the faithful slave she sent,
With message of one word, which meant
But "I remember."
"I love much,"
The Duke sent back. Ah, madness such
As this was never seen. The halls
Of tyrants' palaces have walls
Higher than Love's and Hope's last breath,
Wider than Life, deeper than Death!

Embroidered with a thread of gold
On silk, and hidden fold on fold,
As if an amulet she wore,
Her lover's name the poor Choy bore
By night, by day, upon her heart.
The new slave woman, with an art
As tender as a sister's, sought
To comfort her. Each day she brought
New message from the Duke, each night
Lay at her mistress' feet till light.
O Buddha! pitiful, divine,
All-seeing, gav'st thou no sign
To warn these faithful, loving three,
Who were as faithful unto thee
As to each other! Didst thou teach
The cruel tyrant how to reach
Their life blood, that thy arm might save
Them by the surety of the grave?

Might give to their expiring breath
The gift of life, in shape of death?
Ah, Buddha! pitiful, divine,
Thy gifts of death record no sign
Of life beyond. Our weak hearts crave
Some voice of surety for the grave.

The hours grew ripe: the hour was set,
The night had come. Choy slumbered yet,
While faithful Boon, with footsteps light,
Made all things ready for their flight.
Sudden a clash of arms, — a gleam
Of fire of torches! From her dream
Choy waked, and on her threshold saw,
Dread sight which chilled her blood with awe,
Standing with panting voice and breath,
Maï Taïe, Mother of Death,
Cruelest of all the Amazons,
Slayer of all convicted ones
Who braved the tyrant's wrath and hate.
Choy called on Boon. Too late! too late!
Boon fettered lay with gag and chain;
Most piteous eyes, faithful in pain,
Unto her mistress lifting still.
With blows and jeers wreaking their will,
The soldier women, fierce and strong,
Dragged weeping Choy and Boon along
The by-ways of the silent town,
And flung them, chained and helpless, dowr

Into a dark and loathsome cell.
Soon as their footsteps' echoes fell
Faintly afar, Choy whispered low, —
"O Boon, dear Boon! tell me hast thou
Confessed?"

"Dear Lady, no!" she cried.
"No tortures tyrants ever tried
Shall wring from me one word of blame
Against Phaya Phi Chitt's dear name."
That instant, flashing through Choy's heart
Strange instinct swept.

"Tell me who art
Thou, Boon," she said: "why dost thou cling
To me through all this suffering?
All other women I have known
Had left me now to die alone.
O Boon, conceal from me no more!
Tell me the truth in this dread hour!"
Then, looking newly at her face,
She saw it beauty had, and grace;
Saw that the feet were lithe and fine,
The hands were small and smooth: each sign
Of tender nurture and high blood
This loving woman bore, who stood
To her as slave. Unearthly sweet
Grew Boon's pale face, as to the feet
Of Choy, all crippled, chained, she crept,
And, as she strove to speak, but wept

And sobbed,—
"O Lady dear, forgive
That I deceived thee! I but live
For thy dear Duke. I am his wife!"
Dumb wonder sealed Choy's lips. A strife
Of fierce mistrust warred in her breast.
At last, stern-faced, "Tell me the rest,"
She said.
Closer, more humbly still
Boon crept, and said,—
"Lady, I will;
And, by the heart of Buddha, thou
Canst but forgive when thou dost know
The whole.
"The day my husband came
Home from the fête, he spoke thy name
And told thy beauty unto me,
And said that from that moment he,
His thought, his heart, his blood, were thine,—
Thine utterly, and no more mine
Again. What could I do but weep?
I saw him pine. No food, no sleep,
He took. I thought that he must die.
What could I do? O Lady, I
So loved him that I longed as he
That fate might give him joy and thee.
I vowed to him that I would win
Thee for his wife. How to begin

I knew not, when I found thou wert
The King's last favorite. It hurt
My pride to be a slave. The gold
Lies in the sea for which I sold
Myself to thee, rather than break
My vow. But easy for his sake,
I loved him so, thy service came,
Soon as I found that his dear name
Was dear to thee as thine to him;
That, when I spoke it, it could dim
Thine eyes with passion's tears, like those
Which he had shed in passion's throes,
For want of thee. O Lady, none
Of all thy sighs and tears, not one,
But I have flown and faithful told,
That he might know thou wert not cold.
Each word of beauty, nobleness,
Which thou didst speak, I bore to bless
His heart with knowledge more complete
Of thee. O Lady, the deceit
Was only for his precious sake
And thine: no other way to take
I knew. My husband is so great,
So good, I was but humble mate
For him. As shadow follows shape,
My heart in life cannot escape
From following his; nor yet in death
Shall it be changed: with dying breath,

From Buddha I one joy will wrest,
That he find rapture in thy breast."
Boon ceased, and in her slender hands,
Which scarce could lift her fetter bands,
Buried her face. Choy did not speak.
Her reverence knew not where to seek
For fitting words which she might dare
To use to Boon. The midnight air
Heard only sobs, as close between
Her arms she drew Boon's head to lean
Upon her breast. The long night waned,
And still in silence sat the chained
And helpless women. Strange thoughts filled
The heart of Choy. Her love seemed chilled,
Poor, and untrue, beside this one
Great deed she never could have done.
"Ah, me! his wife has loved him best,"
In bitterness her heart confessed,
Yet jealousy for shame was dead.
Her tears fell loving on Boon's head:
"Dear Boon," she whispered soft and low,
"To Buddha pitiful we go."

Next morning when the judges dread
Cross-questioned Boon, she simply said,
"My Lords, what can a poor slave know?"
Weary at last, the fearful blow
Of lashes on her naked feet
They ordered. Blood ran down the sweet

Soft flesh : still came the answer low,
"My Lords, what can a poor slave know?
Be pitiful!" The swift blows fell
Again : no cry, no sound, to tell
That it was pain, Boon gave ; no sign
Of faltering. They poured down wine
To stay her strength, and then again, —
Oh, surely fiends they were, not men! —
Again, from slender neck to waist,
The cutting blows in angry haste
With tenfold violence they laid.
Each blow a line of red blood made ;
Yet, when they paused, the answer came
Steadfast, heroic, in the same
Pathetic words, more feeble, slow,
"My Lords, what can a poor slave know?"
Then in the torture of the screw,
Whose pain has led strong men to do
Dishonor to their souls and God,
They bound this woman's hands. Sweat stood
In bloody drops along her brow,
Yet from her lips not even now
Was heard one syllable.
In rage,
The baffled tyrants to assuage
Her sufferings tried every art
Which could be tried by kindest heart,
And snatched her back from death again,
Again to tortures fresh ; in vain!

Night came, and from her lips no word
Had fallen. All night they faintly stirred,
As if in sleep she dreamed and spoke.
Choy watching, weeping by her, took
Her hand, and said, —
"Oh, tell thy Choy,
Art thou in mortal pain?"
"My joy
Is greater than my pain," she said,
"That this poor flesh hath not betrayed
My love. Thanking great Buddha now,
I pray unceasing, till we go
Again to torture." Then no more
Boon spoke. To Choy, but little lower
Than angel she appeared. Ah! true
It was the wife loved best! Love knew
His own. His angels comforted
Her soul with joy through hours which bred
But anguish in Choy's breast.
Too soon
Came cruel day, and brought to Boon
Again the lash, the screw; again
Unto the door of death in vain
They tortured her: no word escaped
Her bloodless lips. Her face seemed shaped
Of iron, so calm, so resolute;
A superhuman light her mute
And upward gaze transfigured, till
In awe the torturers stood still.

Then, binding up her wounds, they laid
Her on a couch to rest. New shade
Of anguish now her face revealed,
Waiting Choy's words. All unconcealed,
No doubt, the weaker love lay bare
Before her instinct. It could dare
For self: now that for self remained
No hope, no future to be gained,
Could it for him be true, be great?
Ah, this true torture was, — to wait
Another woman's courage! Eyes
Of fire Boon fixed on Choy. To rise
She helpless strove, in impulse vain,
As if by touch she could sustain
Choy's strength. Her gaze was like a cry.
"Oh, what is death, is suffering, by
The side of truth? If thou dost love
Another, thought of self can move
Thee not. If thou dost love, to bear
The worst is nothing. Dost thou dare
Betray, thou art a coward, liar!"
Entreated, warned Boon's eyes of fire.
They held Choy's eyes as by a spell.
Feeble the judges' stern tones fell,
Idle the threats of torture seemed,
Beside the scorching look which gleamed
Upon that woman's face.
                                        Thus stayed
And stung, Choy bore the blows which laid

Her quivering flesh in furrows. Feet
And neck and shoulders, all the sweet
Fair skin was torn : her blood ran down
As Boon's had run, — not of her own
Resolve, but born of Boon's the strength
Which silent sealed her lips. At length
The one sure pain which torturers know
They tried. No rack, no fire, no blow,
Is dreadful as the screw. At first
Sharp turn it gave, a loud cry burst
From Choy, —
"O Boon, forgive, forgive !
I cannot bear this pain, and live !"
And, shrieking out her lover's name,
She cowered before Boon's eyes of flame.
One cry of uttermost despair
From Boon rang out upon the air,
Her fettered arms above her head
She lifted, and fell back as dead.
Ah ! true it was, the wife loved best !
How true, that cry of Choy's confessed.
To love which she had so betrayed,
No prayer she for forgiveness made :
On him whom she had thought her life
She called not, but upon his wife.

Swift sped the feet of them who sought
The lover. Ere the noon, they brought

Him also. Boon, with anguished eyes,
Beheld him there. She could not rise,
But, creeping on her hands and feet,
She cried, in tones unearthly sweet, —
"O Lords! O Judges! look at me,
And listen. It was I, not he.
I am his wife. I laid the plot.
Except for me, the thought had not
Been his. 'T was only I deceived
The Lady Choy. He but believed
What I desired. The guilt is mine,
All mine. Tell them it was not thine,
My husband, — I can bear the whole."
And, as she turned to him, the soul
Of love ineffable set smile
Upon her face. Her piteous guile,
Transparent, thrilled each heart and ear
That heard her pleading voice. A tear
Fell from the sternest Amazon,
Fierce Khoon Thow App, as in a tone
No mortal from her lips had heard
Before, she said, "O Boon, what stirred
Thy heart to this? Thy motive tell!"
The question all unanswered fell.
Boon lay again as if in death,
With closèd eyes and gasping breath.

All night, low on the dark cell's floor,
Lay Boon and Choy; for Boon no more

Remained in life. When Choy crept near,
And humbly spoke, she answered, " Dear,
Farewell ! " — no other word. Choy strove, —
Poor Choy ! her feebler, lesser love
Avenging on herself its sin, —
Strove from the greater love to win
Some healing stay. Too sweet to pain,
Too loyal and too true to feign,
Boon made but one reply, which fell
Fainter and fainter, " Dear, farewell ! "

That night, at midnight, sat the King
And Lords in council. For the thing
Phaya Phi Chitt and Choy had planned,
Scarcely in all that cruel land
Was known a punishment which seemed
Sufficient. Fierce his red wrath gleamed,
As cried the King, —
" At dawn shall fly
The vultures with their hungry cry.
Rare feast for them ready by noon
Shall be : three traitors' bodies hewn
In pieces, and with offal cast
Abroad, that to the very last
Low grade of life they may return,
And grovel with the beasts to learn,
Through countless ages, in what way
Kings punish when their slaves betray.

Long generations shall forget
Their base-born names, ere souls are set
Again within their foul, false flesh,
To murder love and trust afresh!"[1]

Ah! true it was, the wife loved best!
Love knew his own, gave her his rest;
And, to the other woman, doom
Of life-long woe and life-long gloom.
O cruel friends who prayed the King,
Who dreamed Choy to this world could cling!
Reprieved from death, to life condemned,
Sad prisoner forever hemmed
Within the hated palace-wall;
By all despised, and shunned by all,
Lonely and broken-hearted, she
Weeps day and night in misery.
And day and night one picture haunts
Her weary brain, her sorrow taunts, —
Picture of Buddha's fairest fields,
Where every hour new transport yields,
And where the lover whom she slew,
Loyal at last, and glad and true,
In full Elysium's perfect rest,
Walks with the one who loved him best!

1 The Siamese believe that, whenever a dead body is not burned, its soul is condemned to begin life again in the lowest animal form.

It haunts me morn, and night, and noon:
This story of the woman, Boon, —
Haunts me like restless ghost, that says, —
"Oh, where is love in these sad days!
Rise up, and in my might and name
Plead for the altar and the flame."
I am unworthy: master hands
Should strike the chords, and fill the lands
From sea to sea with melody
Of such transcendent harmony
That it all jubilant might tell
How love must love, if love loves well.
Yet, telling all, and flooding lands
With melody, the master hands
Could strike no deeper chord than I,
When from a woman's heart I cry, —
"O martyred Boon, of peerless fame,
Incarnate in thy life, Love came!"

THE VICTORY OF PATIENCE.

RMED of the gods! Divinest conqueror!
What soundless hosts are thine! Nor pomp, nor state,
Nor token, to betray where thou dost wait.
All Nature stands, for thee, ambassador;
Her forces all thy serfs, for peace or war.
Greatest and least alike, thou rul'st their fate,—
The avalanche chained until its century's date,
The mulberry leaf made robe for emperor!
Shall man alone thy law deny?—refuse
Thy healing for his blunders and his sins?
Oh, make us thine! Teach us who waits best sues;
Who longest waits of all most surely wins.
When Time is spent, Eternity begins.
To doubt, to chafe, to haste, doth God accuse.

GOD'S LIGHT-HOUSES.

HEN night falls on the earth, the sea
From east to west lies twinkling bright
With shining beams from beacons high
Which flash afar a friendly light.

The sailor's eyes, like eyes in prayer,
Turn unto them for guiding ray:
If storms obscure their radiance,
The great ships helpless grope their way.

When night falls on the earth, the sky
Looks like a wide, a boundless main.
Who knows what voyagers sail there?
Who names the ports they seek and gain?

Are not the stars like beacons set
To guide the argosies that go
From universe to universe,
Our little world above, below? —

On their great errands solemn bent,
  In their vast journeys unaware
Of our small planet's name or place
  Revolving in the lower air.

O thought too vast! O thought too glad!
  An awe most rapturous it stirs.
From world to world God's beacons shine:
  God means to save his mariners!

SONGS OF BATTLE.

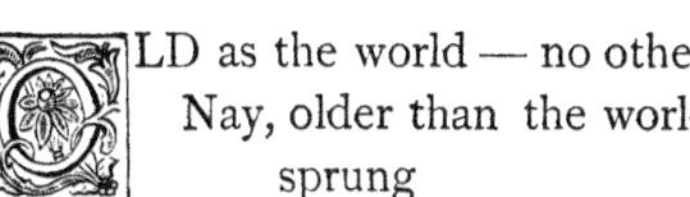

OLD as the world — no other things so old;
Nay, older than the world, else, how had sprung
Such lusty strength in them when earth was young? —
Stand valor and its passion hot and bold,
Insatiate of battle. How, else, told
Blind men, born blind, that red was fitting tongue
Mute, eloquent, to show how trumpets rung
When armies charged and battle-flags unrolled?
Who sings of valor speaks for life, for death,
Beyond all death, and long as life is life,
In rippled waves the eternal air his breath
Eternal bears to stir all noble strife.
Dead Homer from his lost and vanished grave
Keeps battle glorious still and soldiers brave.

NO MAN'S LAND.

WHO called it so? What accident
The wary phase devised?
What wandering fancy thither went,
And lingered there surprised?

Ah, no man's land! O sweet estate
Illimitably fair!
No measure, wall, or bar or gate.
Secure as sky or air.

No greed, no gain; not sold or bought,
Unmarred by name or brand,
Not dreamed of or desired or sought,
Nor visioned, "no man's land."

Suns set and rise, and rise and set,
Whole summers come and go;
And winters pay the summer's debt,
And years of west wind blow;

And harvests of wild seed-times fill,
  And seed and fill again ;
And blossoms bloom at blossoms' will,
  By blossoms overlain ;

And day and night, and night and day,
  Uncounted suns and moons,
By silent shadows mark and stay
  Unreckoned nights and noons :

Ah, "no man's land," hast thou a lover,
  Thy wild, sweet charm who sees?
The stars look down ; the birds fly over ;
  Art thou alone with these?

Ah, "no man's land," when died thy lover,
  Who left no trace to tell?
Thy secret we shall not discover ;
  The centuries keep it well !

JUST OUT OF SIGHT.

I.

N idle reverie, one winter's day,
I watched the narrow vista of a street,
Where crowds of men with noisy, hurrying feet
And eager eyes went on their restless way.
Idly I noted where the boundary lay,
At which the distance did my vision cheat,
Past which each figure fading fast did fleet,
And seem to meet and vanish in the gray.
Sudden there came to me a thought, oft told,
But newly shining then like flash of light, —
"This death, the dread of which turns us so cold,
Outside of our own fears has no stronghold ;
'T is but a boundary, past which, in white,
Our friends are walking still, just out of sight!"

II.

"Just out of sight!" Ay, truly, that is all!
Take comfort in the words, and be deceived
All ye who can, or have not been bereaved!
"Just out of sight." 'T is easy to recall

A face, a voice. O foolish words, and small
And bitter cheer! Men have all this believed,
And yet, in agony, to death have grieved,
For one "just out of sight," beneath a pall!
"Just out of sight." It means the whole of woe:
One sudden stricken blind who loved the light;
One starved where he had feasted day and night;
One who was crowned, to beggary brought low;
All this death doeth, going to and fro
And putting those we love "just out of sight."

SEPTEMBER WOODS.

GIRT round by meadows wearing shabby
weeds
For clover's early death, and sentried by
The tireless locust, with his muffled click
Of secret weapon, at each footfall, stand
The woods.
September, smiling treacherous smiles,
And bearing in his hand a hollow truce
Which gentle Summer trusts, can enter free.
O fatal trust! Her sacred inner court
Of Holies, holiest, the lovely queen
Throws open to the ally of her foe.
By day, with sunny look and gracious air
He wins her heart and wears her colors. Night
Beholds him, in his white and gleaming mail,
Alert and noiseless, following the dews,
Her faithful messengers, waylaying them
With sudden cruel death, and, in their stead,
His own foul treason bearing through the realm.
Lured by his guile, the green and twining vines
Array themselves in party-colored robes
And loosely flaunt, unknowing 't is their death.

The low Bunch-Berry her nun's white lays by,
And wearing claret satin, decks her breast
With knots of scarlet beads. This sin, O sweet,
In resurrection of the coming Spring,
Shall be forgiven thee, and thou again
Shalt rise, as white as snow.
The fragrant ferns,
And clinging mosses, to whom Summer kind
Had been, more than to other lowly things,
Are true; and not till they are trampled low
By icy warriors, will they refuse
Their emerald carpet to her tread, and then,
In cold white grief, will die around her feet:
The simpering Birch, unstable in the wind,
Is first to break his faith, and cheaply bought
By gold, in brazen vanity, lifts up
His arms, and broadly waves the glittering price
Of his dishonor: Poplars next and Elms
Grow envious of the yellow show, and hold
Their hands for traitor's wages; but more scant
And dim the golden tokens gained by them;
For now disloyalty has spread, and grown
More bold of front: whole clans are cheaply won.
In hostile signal fires from hill to hill,
The Maples blaze; the tangling Sumach-trees
Of glowing spikes build crimson ladders up
The wall; ungainly Moosewood strives and creeps
And shakes his purple-spotted banner out
Defiantly; the sturdy Beeches throw

Their harvest down, and bristle in a suit
Of leathern points : all is revolt, and all
Is lost for Summer !

Vainly now she showers
By brook and pool her white and purple stars,
And lifts in all the fields her Golden-Rod ;
In vain thin scarlet streamers sets along
The meadows, and to Gentian's pallid lips
Of blue calls back the chilled and torpid bee ;
Sweet queen, her kingdom rocks ! Her only stay
And comfort now, the loving Pines who wait
In solemn grief, unmoved and undismayed
By guile or threats, and to their farthest kin,
A haughty and untarnished race, will keep
Eternally inviolate and green
Their sworn allegiance to her and all
Her name ! Encircled by their arms she dies ;
And not the deadliest thrusts of wintry spears,
Nor sweeping avalanche of snow and ice,
Can daunt them from their silent watch around
Her sepulchre, nor from their faithful hold
Can wrest the babe, who, hid in sacred depths
And fed on sacred food, and nurtured till
The fated day, shall lift her infant hand,
And slaying the usurper, take the throne
Next in the royal line of summer queens.

TO-DAY.

 SADDEST prisoner, to death condemned,
Going blindfold, with slow, reluctant feet,
Hands fettered and mute lips, thy doom
to meet,
By flaming swords before, behind thee, hemmed,
Led by two Fates, — To-morrow, with her gemmed
Arms that flash mocking tokens of the sweet
Things thou hadst hoped ; and Yesterday with cheat
Of withered roses which thou hast contemned,
Decking her icy brow and heavy pall ;
While we, mute, helpless, with prophetic black
Have wrapped ourselves, and in thy narrow track
Come, hand in hand, blindfolded, fettered all,
Waiting the hour when, in thy death's last thrall
Bidding us follow thee, thou shalt look back.

OPPORTUNITY.

DO not know if, climbing some steep hill,
Through fragrant wooded pass, this glimpse
I bought,
Or whether in some mid-day I was caught
To upper air, where visions of God's will
In pictures to our quickened sense fulfil
His word. But this I saw.
A path I sought
Through wall of rock. No human fingers wrought
The golden gates which opened sudden, still,
And wide. My fear was hushed by my delight.
Surpassing fair the lands; my path lay plain;
Alas, so spell-bound, feasting on the sight,
I paused, that I but reached the threshold bright,
When, swinging swift, the golden gates again
Were rocky wall, by which I wept in vain.

FLOWERS ON A GRAVE.

I.

WHAT sweeter thing to hear, through tears,
than this,
Of one who dies, that, looking on him
dead,
All men with tender reverence gazed and said:
"What courtesy and gentleness were his!
Our ruder lives, for years to come, will miss
His sweet serenity, which daily shed
A grace we scarcely felt, so deep inbred
Of nature was it. Loyalty which is
So loyal as his loyalty to friends
Is rare; such purity is rarer still."
Yes, there is yet one sweeter thing. It ends
The broken speech with sobs that choke and fill
Our throats.
Alas! lost friend, we knew not how
Our hearts were won to love thee, until now.

II.

SOME lives are bright like torches, and their flame
Casts flickering lights around, and changeful heats;
Some lives blaze like the meteor which fleets
Across the sky; and some of lofty aim

Stand out like beacon-lights. But never came,
Or can, a light so satisfying sweet,
As steady daylight, unperturbed, complete,
And noiseless.
Human lives we see the same
As this; their equilibrium so just,
Their movement so serene, so still, small heed
The world pays to their presence till in need
It sudden finds itself. The darkness near,
The precious life returning dust for dust,
It recollects how noon and life were clear.

III.

How poor is all that fame can be or bring!
Although a generation feed the pyre,
How soon dies out the lifeless, loveless fire!
The king is dead. Hurrah! Long live the king!
The poet breathes his last. Who next will sing?
The great man falls. Who comes to mount still higher?
Oh, bitter emptiness of such desire!
Earth holds but one true good, but one true thing,
And this is it — to walk in honest ways
And patient, and with all one's heart belong
In love unto one's own! No death so strong
That life like this he ever conquers, slays;
The centuries do to it no hurt, no wrong:
They are eternal resurrection days.

A MEASURE OF HOURS.

NTO those two I called who hold
In hands omnipotent all lives
Of men, and deal, like gods, such doled
Alms as they list, to him who strives
And him who waits alike:

"Oh! show
Me but how measure ye one hour
Of time, that I at least may know
If I lift up this cross what power
I need; and what I win of bliss
If I may dare to pay the cost —
Whole cost, without which I must miss
This joy, and feel my life lost."
Then Joy spoke first, all breathless:

"Drink!
An hour seems like eternity.
My moments hold whole ages. Think
No price too great which buys for thee
This boundless bliss. Such hours as mine

Mock reckonings. The sands stand still.
Drink quickly! I will give the sign
When it is over. Drink thy fill!"

I had scarce tasted when, with face
All changed and voice grown sharp, Joy cried:
"Thine hour is past. Give place! Give place!
New hearts impatiently abide
Thy going. Every man fills up
His own swift measure. Thou hadst thine.
Who weakly drains the empty cup
Drinks only bitter dregs of wine."

Then Sorrow whispered gently: "Take
This burden up. Be not afraid.
An hour is short. Thou scarce wilt wake
To consciousness that I have laid
My hand upon thee, when the hour
Shall all have passed, and, gladder then
For the brief pain's uplifting power,
Thou shalt but pity griefless men."

I grew by minutes changed and old,
As men change not in many years
Of happiness. Lifetimes untold
Seemed dragging lifeless by. My tears
Ran slow for utter weariness
Of weeping; and, when token came

The hour was done, I felt far less
Of joy than woe; as one whose name
Is called, when prison doors have swung
Open too late, reluctantly
Goes forth to find himself among
Strange faces, desolate, though free.

"O cruel brethren, Joy and Grief,"
I cried, "with equal mockery
Your promises meet our belief.
One blossom and one fruit will be
Your harvest! But full well I know
They are not harvest; only seed
Sown in our tears, from which shall grow
In other soil harvest indeed, —

"Harvest in God's great gardens white,
Where cool and living waters run,
And where the spotless Lamb is light,
Instead of pallid moon and sun;
Where constant through the golden air
The tree of life sheds mystic leaf,
Which angels to the nations bear,
Healing alike their joy and grief."

CHARLOTTE CUSHMAN.

I.

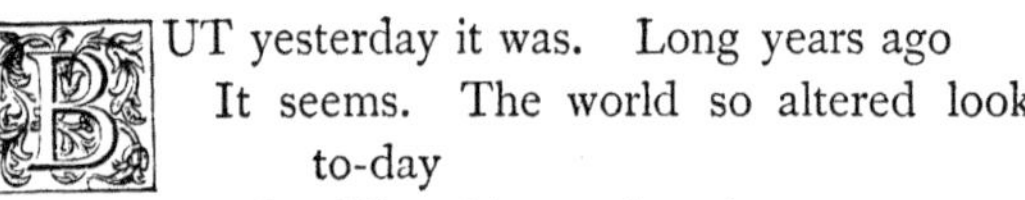
BUT yesterday it was. Long years ago
It seems. The world so altered looks to-day
That, journeying idly with my thoughts astray,
I gazed where rose one lofty peak of snow
Above grand tiers on tiers of peaks below.
One moment brief it shone, then sank away,
As swift we reached a point where foot-hills lay
So near they seemed like mountains huge to grow,
And touch the sky. That instant, idly still,
My eye fell on a printed line, and read
Incredulous, with sudden anguished thrill,
The name of this great queen among the dead.
I raised my eyes. The dusty foot-hills near
Had gone. Again the snowy peak shone clear.

II.

OH ! thou beloved woman, soul and heart
And life, thou standest unapproached and grand,
As still that glorious snowy peak doth stand.
The dusty barrier our clumsy art

In terror hath called death holds thee apart
From us. 'T is but the low foot-hill of sand
Which bars our vision in a mountain-land.
One moment further on, and we shall start
With speechless joy to find that we have passed
The dusky mound which shuts us from the light
Of thy great love, still quick and warm and fast,
Of thy great strengths, heroically cast,
Of thy great soul, still glowing pure and white,
Of thy great life, still pauseless, full, and bright!

DEDICATION.

SAW men kneeling where their hands had brought
And fashioned curiously a pile of stone.
To God they said they gave it, for his own,
And that their psalms and prayers had wrought
Its consecration. When, perplexed, I sought
Their meaning, they but answered with a groan,
And called my question blasphemy. Alone,
In silence of the wilderness, I thought
Again. Swift answer came from rock, tree, sod:
"These puny prayers superfluous rise, and late
These psalms. When first the world swung out in space,
Amid the shoutings of the sons of God,
Then was its every atom dedicate,
Forever holy by God's gift and grace."

DAWN.

ITH a ring of silver,
And a ring of gold,
And a red, red rose
Which illumines her face,
The sun, like a lover
Who glows and is bold,
Wooes the lovely earth
To his strong embrace.

EVE.

N millions of pieces
The beautiful rings
And the scattered petals
Of the rose so red,
The sun, like a lover
Who is weary, flings
On the lonely earth
When the day is dead.

DREAMS.

MYSTERIOUS shapes, with wands of joy and pain,
Which seize us unaware in helpless sleep,
And lead us to the houses where we keep
Our secrets hid, well barred by every chain
That we can forge and bind: the crime whose stain
Is slowly fading 'neath the tears we weep;
Dead bliss which, dead, can make our pulses leap —
Oh, cruelty! To make these live again!
They say that death is sleep, and heaven's rest
Ends earth's short day, as, on the last faint gleam
Of sun, our nights shut down, and we are blest.
Let this, then, be of heaven's joy the test,
The proof if heaven be, or only seem,
That we forever choose what we will dream!

THE DAY-STAR IN THE EAST.

I.

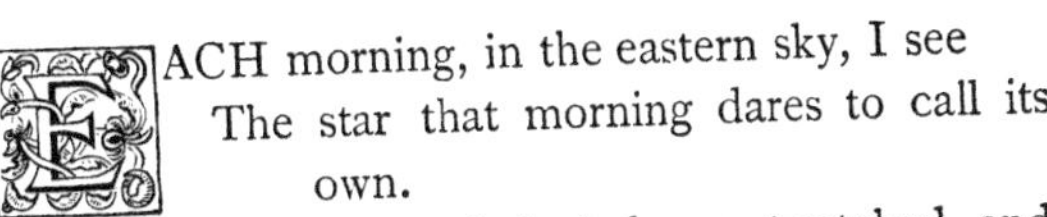ACH morning, in the eastern sky, I see
The star that morning dares to call its own.
Night's myriads it has outwatched and outshone;
Full radiant dawn pales not its majesty;
Peer of the sun, his herald fit and free.
Sudden from earth, dark, heavy mists are blown;
The city's grimy smoke, to pillars grown,
Climbs up the sky, and hides the star from me.
Strange, that a film of smoke can blot a star!
On comes, with blinding glare, the breathless day:
The star is gone. The moon doth surer lay
Than midnight gloom, athwart its light, a bar.
But steadfast as God's angels planets are.
To-morrow's dawn will show its changeless ray.

II.

THE centuries are God's days; within his hand,
Held in the hollow, as a balance swings,
Less than its dust, are all our temporal things.
Long are his nights, when darkness steeps the land;

Thousands of years fill one slow dawn's demand ;
The human calendar its measure brings,
Feeble and vain, to lift the soul that clings
To hope for light, and seeks to understand.
The centuries are God's days ; the greatest least
In his esteem. We have no glass to sweep
His universe. A hand's-breadth distant dies,
To our poor ears, the strain whose echoes keep
All heaven glad. We do but grope and creep.
There always is a day-star in the skies !

OCTOBER'S BRIGHT BLUE WEATHER.

SUNS and skies and clouds of June,
And flowers of June together,
Ye cannot rival for one hour
October's bright blue weather,

When loud the bumble-bee makes haste,
Belated, thriftless vagrant,
And golden-rod is dying fast,
And lanes with grapes are fragrant;

When gentians roll their fringes tight
To save them for the morning,
And chestnuts fall from satin burrs
Without a sound of warning;

When on the ground red apples lie
In piles like jewels shining,
And redder still on old stone walls
Are leaves of woodbine twining;

When all the lovely wayside things
  Their white-winged seeds are sowing,
And in the fields, still green and fair,
  Late aftermaths are growing;

When springs run low, and on the brooks,
  In idle golden freighting,
Bright leaves sink noiseless in the hush
  Of woods, for winter waiting;

When comrades seek sweet country haunts,
  By twos and twos together,
And count like misers hour by hour,
  October's bright blue weather.

O suns and skies and flowers of June,
  Count all your boasts together,
Love loveth best of all the year
  October's bright blue weather.

THE RIVIERA.

O PEERLESS shore of peerless sea,
Ere mortal eye had gazed on thee,
What god was lover first of thine,
Drank deep of thy unvintaged wine,
And lying on thy shining breast
Knew all thy passion and thy rest;
And when thy love he must resign,
O generous god, first love of thine,
Left such a dower of wealth to thee,
Thou peerless shore of peerless sea!
Thy balmy air, thy stintless sun,
Thy orange-flowering never done,
Thy myrtle, olive, palm, and pine,
Thy golden figs, thy ruddy wine,
Thy subtle and resistless spell
Which all men feel and none can tell?
O peerless shore of peerless sea!
From all the world we turn to thee;
No wonder deem we thee divine!
Some god was lover first of thine.

SEMITONES.

H me, the subtle boundary between
What pleases and what pains! The difference
Between the word that thrills our every sense
With joy and one which hurts, although it mean
No hurt! It is the things that are unseen,
Invisible, not things of violence,
For which the mightiest are without defence.
On kine most fair to see one may grow lean
With hunger. Many a snowy bread is doled
Which is far harder than the hardest stones.
'T is but a narrow line divides the zones
Where suns are warm from those where suns are cold.
'Twixt harmonies divine as chords can hold
And torturing discords, lie but semitones!

IN THE DARK.

AS one who journeys on a stormy night
Through mountain passes which he does not know
Shields like his life from savage gusts that blow
The swaying flame of his frail torch's light,
So each of us through life's long groping fight
Clings fast to one dear faith, one love, whose glow
Makes darkness noonday to our trusting sight,
And joys of perils into which we go.
God help us, when this precious shining mark
The raging storms of deep distrust assail
With icy, poisoned breath and deadly aim,
Till we, with hearts that shrink and cower and quail
In terror which no measure has nor name,
Stand trembling, helpless, palsied, in the dark.

MORDECAI.

AKE friends with him! He is of royal line,
Although he sits in rags. Not all of thine
Array of splendor, pomp of high estate,
Can buy him from his place within the gate,
The King's Gate of thy happiness, where he,
Yes, even he, the Jew, remaineth free,
Never obeisance making, never scorn
Betraying of thy silver and new-born
Delight. Make friends with him, for unawares
The charmèd secret of thy joys he bears;
Be glad, so long as his black sackcloth, late
And early, thwarts thy sun; for if in hate
And haste thou plottest for his blood, thy own death-cry,
Not his, comes from the gallows fifty cubits high.

IN APRIL.

WHAT did the sparrow do yesterday?
Nobody knew but the sparrows;
He were too bold who should try to say;
They have forgotten it all to-day.
Why does it haunt my thoughts this way,
With a joy that piques and harrows,
As the birds fly past,
And the chimes ring fast,
And the long spring shadows sweet shadow cast?

There 's a maple-bud redder to-day;
It will almost flower to-morrow;
I could swear 't was only yesterday
In a sheath of snow and ice it lay,
With fierce winds blowing it every way;
Whose surety had it to borrow,
Till birds should fly past,
And chimes ring fast,
And the long spring shadows sweet shadow cast?

"Was there ever a day like to-day,
  So clear, so shining, so tender?"
The old cry out; and the children say,
With a laugh, aside: "That 's always the way
With the old, in spring; as long as they stay,
  They find in it greater splendor,
    When the birds fly past,
    And the chimes ring fast,
And the long spring shadows sweet shadow cast!"

Then that may be why my thoughts all day —
  I see I am old, by the token —
Are so haunted by sounds, now sad, now gay,
Of the words I hear the sparrows say,
And the maple-bud's mysterious way
  By which from its sheath it has broken,
    While the birds fly past,
    And the chimes ring fast,
And the long spring shadows sweet shadow cast!

TWO HARVESTS.

I.

BLOSSOM and fruit no man could count or
hoard;
Seasons their laws forgot, in riot haste
Lavishing yield on yield in madman's waste;
No tropic with its centuries' heat outpoured
In centuries of summers, ever stored
Such harvest.
Had the earth her sole pearl placed
In wine of sun to melt, — one blissful taste
To drain and die, — it had not fully dowered
This harvest!
She who smiling goes, a queen,
Reaping with alabaster arms and hands
The fruits and flowers of these magic lands,
With idle, satiate intervals between, —
Oh, what to her do laws of harvest mean?
Joy passes by her, where she laden stands!

II.

A PARCHED and arid land, all colorless,
Than desert drearier, than rock more stern;
Spring could not find, nor any summer learn
The secret to redeem this wilderness.
Harsh winds sweep through with icy storm and stress:
Fierce lurid suns shine but to blight and burn;
And streams rise, pallid, but to flee and turn:
Who soweth here waits miracle to bless
The harvest!
She who smiling goes, a queen,
Seeking with hidden tears and tireless hands
To win a fruitage from these barren lands, —
She knoweth what the laws of harvest mean!
Blades spring, flowers bloom, by all but her unseen;
Joy's halo crowns her, where she patient stands!

HABEAS CORPUS.

MY body, eh? Friend Death, how now?
Why all this tedious pomp of writ?
Thou hast reclaimed it sure and slow
For half a century, bit by bit.

In faith thou knowest more to-day
Than I do, where it can be found!
This shrivelled lump of suffering clay,
To which I now am chained and bound,

Has not of kith or kin a trace
To the good body once I bore;
Look at this shrunken, ghastly face:
Didst ever see that face before?

Ah, well, friend Death, good friend thou art;
Thy only fault thy lagging gait,
Mistaken pity in thy heart
For timorous ones that bid thee wait.

Do quickly all thou hast to do,
  Nor I nor mine will hindrance make ;
I shall be free when thou art through ;
  I grudge thee nought that thou must take !

Stay ! I have lied ; I grudge thee one,
  Yes, two I grudge thee at this last, —
Two members which have faithful done
  My will and bidding in the past.

I grudge thee this right hand of mine ;
  I grudge thee this quick-beating heart ;
They never gave me coward sign,
  Nor played me once a traitor's part.

I see now why in olden days
  Men in barbaric love or hate
Nailed enemies' hands at wild crossways,
  Shrined leaders' hearts in costly state :

The symbol, sign, and instrument
  Of each soul's purpose, passion, strife,
Of fires in which are poured and spent
  Their all of love, their all of life.

O feeble, mighty human hand !
  O fragile, dauntless human heart !
The universe holds nothing planned
  With such sublime, transcendent art !

Yes, Death, I own I grudge thee mine
  Poor little hand, so feeble now;
Its wrinkled palm, its altered line,
  Its veins so pallid and so slow —

. . . (Unfinished here.)

Ah, well, friend Death, good friend thou art;
  I shall be free when thou art through.
Take all there is — take hand and heart;
  There must be somewhere work to do.

A LAST PRAYER.

ATHER, I scarcely dare to pray,
So clear I see, now it is done,
That I have wasted half my day,
And left my work but just begun;

So clear I see that things I thought
Were right or harmless were a sin;
So clear I see that I have sought,
Unconscious, selfish aims to win;

So clear I see that I have hurt
The souls I might have helped to save;
That I have slothful been, inert,
Deaf to the calls thy leaders gave.

In outskirts of thy kingdoms vast,
Father, the humblest spot give me;
Set me the lowliest task thou hast;
Let me repentant work for thee!

THE SONG HE NEVER WROTE.

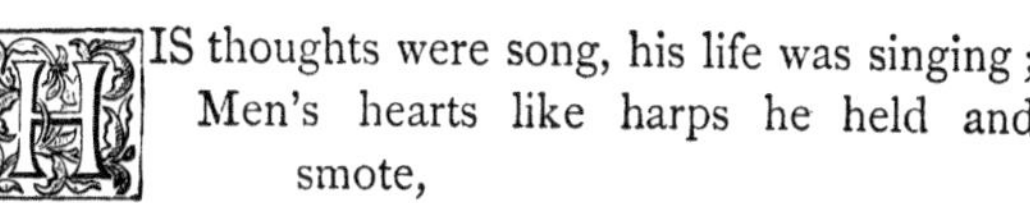

HIS thoughts were song, his life was singing;
  Men's hearts like harps he held and smote,
But in his heart went ever ringing,
  Ringing, the song he never wrote.

Hovering, pausing, luring, fleeting,
  A farther blue, a brighter mote,
The vanished sound of swift winds meeting,
  The opal swept beneath the boat.

A gleam of wings forever flaming,
  Never folded in nest or cote;
Secrets of joy, past name or naming;
  Measures of bliss past dole or rote;

Echoes of music, always flying,
  Always echo, never the note;
Pulses of life, past life, past dying,—
  All these in the song he never wrote.

Dead at last, and the people, weeping,
Turned from his grave with wringing hands, —
"What shall we do, now he lies sleeping,
His sweet song silent in our lands?

"Just as his voice grew clearer, stronger," —
This was the thought that keenest smote, —
"O Death! couldst thou not spare him longer?
Alas for the songs he never wrote!"

Free at last, and his soul up-soaring,
Planets and skies beneath his feet,
Wonder and rapture all out-pouring,
Eternity how simple, sweet!

Sorrow slain, and every regretting,
Love and Love's labors left the same,
Weariness over, suns without setting,
Motion like thought on wings of flame:

Higher the singer rose and higher,
Heavens, in spaces, sank like bars;
Great joy within him glowed like fire,
He tossed his arms among the stars, —

"This is the life, past life, past dying;
I am I, and I live the life:
Shame on the thought of mortal crying!
Shame on its petty toil and strife!

"Why did I halt, and weakly tremble?"
Even in heaven the memory smote,—
"Fool to be dumb, and to dissemble!
Alas for the song I never wrote!"

www.ingramcontent.com/pod-product-compliance
Lightning Source LLC
LaVergne TN
LVHW021414110826
845150LV00007B/1924

* 9 7 8 1 4 2 5 5 1 0 1 7 6 *